ONONDAGA COUNTY
PUBLIC LIBRARY

IN MEMORY OF

John "Jack" Collins

FROM

THE LADIES OF THE CLUB

2002

Covered Bridges
of
New York State

A Guide

RICK L. BERFIELD

Photographs by Richard R. Wilson

SYRACUSE UNIVERSITY PRESS

First Edition 2003
03 04 05 06 07 08   6 5 4 3 2 1

The paper used in this publication meets the minimum requirements
of American National Standard for Information Sciences—
Permanence of Paper for Printed Library Materials, ANSI Z39.48–1984.∞™

Library of Congress Cataloging-in-Publication Data
Berfield, Rick L.
Covered bridges of New York State : a guide / Rick L. Berfield ;
photographs by Richard R. Wilson.—1st ed.
p. cm.
ISBN 0–8156–0748–2 (alk. paper)
1. Covered bridges—New York (State) 2. Bridges—New York (State) I.
Title.
TG24.N7 N48 2003
624'.2—dc21
2002151866

Printed in Canada

Contents

Illustrations

Figures

Rick L. Berfield earned a bachelor of science degree in civil engineering from Ohio State University in 1985. He worked as a structural engineer and bridge designer for the New York State Department of Transportation for ten years and possesses a current professional engineer's license. Rick is a lifetime member of the New York State Covered Bridge Society and of the National Society for the Preservation of Covered Bridges. He now resides in New Smyrna Beach, Florida.

Preface

MY INTEREST IN COVERED BRIDGES began when I discovered an atlas showing their locations throughout Pennsylvania. Much to my surprise, I learned that Pennsylvania has more covered bridges than any other state. The Keystone State has more covered bridges than any other country in the world! I traveled to my first covered bridge after carefully mapping out a "bridging" route of Sullivan and Columbia Counties, Pennsylvania. The Sonestown Covered Bridge, painted barn red, is a beautiful rustic structure that spans Muncy Creek. The foliage was at a perfect peak and the autumn day was all sunshine. I visited five more bridges that day and unfortunately ran out of film. This adventure sparked my passion for covered bridges. I made several more trips to visit Pennsylvania covered bridges, but began to wonder how many were located in New York State.

My occupation as a civil engineer and bridge designer made it hard for me to stay away from covered bridges. My supervisor soon learned of my newfound interest and gave me a pamphlet on covered bridges in New York State. I was amazed. There are only twenty-four historic covered bridges, older than fifty years, remaining in New York State. The Jay Covered Bridge has been dismantled but is slated for restoration beginning in 2003. Four other covered bridges (Tuscarora Club, Lower Shavertown, Copeland, and Ashokan/ Turnwood) are on private land and require special permission to visit. Originally these five bridges were not going to be included. But after meeting several friends along the way and receiving strong backing from the guide's architectural historian, Mr. Richard Wilson, president of the New York State Covered Bridge Society, it was possible to include a detailed review of all twenty-four bridges.

Statistics and field observation notes were recorded from the fall of 1997 through the fall of 1999. Hamden Covered Bridge was recorded a second time after its restoration on August 27, 2001. The name of the covered bridge, county, year built, truss system, roadway carried, waterway crossed, number of spans, length, and "covered bridge assigned number" were documented in the *World Guide to Covered Bridges* (1989) and verified in the field. Clear width, out-to-out width, and clearance measurements were recorded to the nearest inch. However, some inaccuracies may be found due to the fact that I measured both portals of each covered bridge and often found them to differ. I personally recorded all statistics, field observation notes, measurements, and drawings.

I hope you receive as much enjoyment reading this book as I found writing it—happy bridging!

■　■　■

At one time there were more than 250 covered bridges throughout New York State, but the forces of nature and the destruction of them by humanity have eliminated all but a handful. The historic twenty-four covered bridges found in this guide are all over fifty years old, spanning the years between 1823 and 1912. Although the number may seem few, a person would need to travel several miles to see all the bridges. One might find a ride in the country relaxing to enjoy these romantic symbols of the past. It would not be an oddity to drive or stroll through a covered bridge built before the Civil War. Perhaps one would like to capture that "perfect" setting on film or maybe just cast in a line to see if the native trout are biting. For whatever reason, covered bridges still lure attention today as they did years ago.

In years past, a covered bridge that had no openings other than the portals provided a dark and romantic shelter where a gentleman suitor could steal a kiss from his sweetheart. "Kissing bridges" became favorite landmarks for many events. Baptisms, weddings, and funeral ceremonies were commonly held near covered bridges. A tradition among young and old is to adorn the gables with wreaths to celebrate the holiday season. Several covered bridges became toll bridges and were part of the early turnpike system. Toll keepers adjusted the tolls depending upon the livestock and number of people crossing. Unfortunately, the toll payer and the toll keeper did not always agree. Traveling salespersons would frequent the bridges to post advertisements on the timbers and rafters. Some tattered remains of endorsements posted inside covered bridges can still be found today.

During horse-and-buggy times, wood was abundant, nearby, strong, and an inexpensive resource for building bridges. Some of the earliest timber bridges were left uncovered, but soon deteriorated from exposure to the weather. The invention of the truss, or supportive framework, allowed wooden bridges to span longer distances. The trusses were also open to the elements and soon rotted and decayed. Bridge builders found that flooring and siding were easily replaceable, but trusses were not. Covering the trusses with a roof became the likely solution—hence, the birth of the covered bridge.

Historic New York State covered bridges proudly exhibit a wide variety of truss designs. Each design is a rigid framework of timbers or timbers and bars, usually in a triangular pattern, used to support the bridge. The triangle is the only geometric shape that will not distort under loading without first failing at one of the joints. Truss systems constitute each side of a covered bridge and provide the strength for the structure. The following is a summary of the historic New York State truss systems still in existence. (See individual truss diagrams in the chapters that follow for proportional drawings.)

Long

The Hamden bridge utilizes the Long's Panel truss, constructed from crossing diagonal timbers separated by vertical timbers. The distance between the centers of the vertical timbers constitutes one panel.

Queenpost

The Queenpost truss of the Copeland bridge is formed by diagonal timbers that slope outward from top to bottom and are connected by a horizontal timber or timbers at the top.

Long with Queenpost

The Downsville bridge combines the Long and Queenpost systems.

Town Lattice

The Town Lattice truss is constructed from parallel diagonal timbers in one direction joined by parallel diagonal timbers in the opposite direction. Where the timbers cross, a joint is formed by drilling through both timbers and inserting a wooden pin called a trunnel or "treenail." Fitch's, Lower Shavertown, Halls Mills, Beaverkill, Bendo, Ashokan/Turnwood, Grants Mills, Eagleville, and Shushan Covered Bridges all use the Town Lattice truss.

Howe

The Howe truss can be found in the Jay, Rexleigh, and Buskirk bridges. It is similar to the Long's Panel truss, but iron tie rods comprise the vertical members.

Burr

The Burr Arch is formed by curved segments of hewn timber that rest on both abutments, as found in Hyde Hall and Perrine's bridges.

Multiple Kingpost and Arch

The Salisbury Center bridge is constructed from the Burr Arch design in conjunction with diagonal sloping timbers separated by vertical timbers. The diagonal timbers slope outward from top to bottom away from a center kingpost.

Long and Center Arch

The Blenheim bridge combines the Long's Panel and Burr Arch systems.

Town and Laminated Arch

The Van Tran Flat and Newfield bridges have the Town Lattice truss along with the Laminated Arch, which is formed by glue-laminating several wooden planks together to form curved segments that rest on both abutments.

Kingpost

The Kingpost truss is constructed from two diagonal timbers that slope outward from top to bottom away from a center kingpost, and can be seen in the Forge and Tappan bridges.

Two notable truss designers who had a profound impact on building New York State covered bridges were Theodore Burr and Ithiel Town. Burr and Town left a lasting impression on these covered bridges because several of the truss designs remaining today have used their patents. Theodore Burr, a native of Torringford, Connecticut, began his career in New York and patented the Burr truss in 1817. Ithiel Town, a native of Bridgeport, Connecticut, patented the first Town Lattice truss on January 1, 1820, as a simple lattice. In 1835, he patented another Town Lattice truss that had secondary chords (horizontal truss timbers) added to his original design.

Sixteen of the bridges in this book are on the National Register of Historic Places, the official listing of buildings, structures, districts, objects, and sites significant in the history, architecture, archaeology, and culture of the United States (United States National Park Service 2000). See Appendix C for a list of these bridges and the dates they were chosen for the Register.

Delaware County (western Catskills) has five historic covered bridges remaining. Downsville Covered Bridge, built in 1854, is the oldest covered bridge in the county and the third longest in New York State at 174 feet. Robert Murray was the builder of this bridge at a cost of $1700. Long truss designs are rare to northeastern covered bridges, and this one is the only historic New York State covered bridge that uses a Long with Queenpost truss design. Flying buttresses (sway bracing beyond) provide lateral support and prevent the structure from leaning or twisting under transverse loads such as wind, ice, and water. The design was frequently used in the Catskill region. This was once a meeting place where immersion baptisms took place in the East Branch of the Delaware River. The bridge underwent a restoration in the fall of 1998 and reopened to traffic in the spring of 1999. Restoration included installation of the longest glue-laminated wood beams in the country at 174 feet (Rinda 1999, 3). On May 22, 1999, the first annual Colchester Covered Bridge Festival was held. Events included a trout fishing derby, a five-kilometer running race, street fairs and demonstrations, a parade, a concert by the Catskill Symphony Orchestra, a block party, and fireworks (Guay 1999, 6). This location of-

fers free public parking, fishing access, a canoe launch, and a picnic area that includes a lighted gazebo.

Fitch's Covered Bridge is one of nine Town Lattice truss designs. This design was unique because braces were tied into the vertical endposts and radiated, or "fanned," toward the opposite end of each truss. The radiating braces are common among Catskill Town Lattice trusses. The bridge was originally constructed in 1870 in Delhi on Kingston Street and moved three miles upstream by David L. Wright in 1885. During the move, the bridge was turned 180 degrees and now faces in the opposite direction (McKee 1997, 64). Consequently, timbers labeled "east," are placed on the west bank of the West Branch of the Delaware River, and those marked "west" rest on the east shore (Galusha 1989, 8). Fitch's Covered Bridge was rehabilitated in 2001. The work included lengthening the bridge to its original length of 114 feet, rebuilding the trusses to eliminate the radiating braces, eliminating the flying buttresses, adding three diamond-shaped windows to each side, installing a wooden-shingled roof, and installing natural wood siding on the sides and portals.

Hamden Covered Bridge was built by Robert Murray in 1859 at a cost of $1000. A center pier was added in the 1940s to support the single span (Wilson 1991a, 14). "Robert Murray is New York State's contribution to the Hall of Fame of covered bridge builders," wrote Richard Sanders Allen in November 1943. Murray built nine recorded covered bridges throughout Delaware County (Herrmann 1974, 42). The bridge at Hamden is built solely with Long trusses, the last of this type remaining in New York State. Two windows were added to each side in 1966 to allow fishing access from the bridge and to help deter children from knocking sideboards loose (Herrmann 1974, 42). In the summer of 2000, a crane tipped while attempting to dismantle the bridge, causing the top chord to fail. One-third of the structure was lowered into the West Branch of the Delaware River. Hamden Covered Bridge is now completely restored with a single 130-foot glue-laminated chord, lengthwise deck planking, and natural wood siding on the sides and portals. The pier and flying buttresses were eliminated.

Tuscarora Club Covered Bridge was originally built in Dunraven in 1870 by William Mead. It spanned thirty-eight feet over the Platte Kill Stream using a Queenpost truss design. This bridge once served as a tollgate bridge. In 1935 Albert Rosa, superintendent of the Town of Middletown, sold the structure to Turner Barr, an active member of the Tuscarora Club, and the bridge was moved to the fishing club grounds. The bridge was reconstructed as a Kingpost truss design and placed over Mill Brook at the head of "Demis Hole." A severe freshet nearly removed the bridge from its foundation. The bridge was set on a firmer foundation, the roof was shingled, and the channel was enlarged (Herrmann 1974, 108, 110–11). This bridge is no longer a true "truss" bridge and is now considered a "stringer" bridge. Tuscarora Club Covered Bridge is privately owned by a men's hunting and fishing club whose members do not wish to have visitors.

Lower Shavertown Covered Bridge now spans thirty-two feet across Trout Brook and uses a Town Lattice truss design. This is the second-smallest length of the New York State historic covered bridges. It was built in 1877 by Anson Jenkins and August Neidig of Union Grove, N.Y. Originally, the bridge spanned fifty-four feet across Lew Beach Hill Brook in Lower Shavertown. Instead of the floor beams resting on the bottom chord, they were hung from under the chord to provide greater vertical clearance. In 1954, construction began on the Pepacton Reservoir and the bridge was moved to Carl Campbell's private land. The structure became known as Campbell's Covered Bridge and served as an entranceway to his lodge. Mr. Campbell has since passed away and the new owners have reinstated the Lower Shavertown name, but it is still a private bridge (Wilson 1991b, 8).

Essex County (northern Adirondacks) has a single historic covered bridge remaining. The Jay Covered Bridge was built in 1857 by George M. Burt of AuSable Forks. He used a Howe truss design that included iron tie rods and bearing blocks as an inverted "T." It is believed that the blocks were patented by Reuben Comins from Troy, N.Y. on February 10, 1857 (Wells 1996, 3). The single-span bridge was 175 feet long and had four piers added for support in the 1950s (Wilson 1991a, 16). This was the second-longest of the twenty-four remaining New York State historic covered bridges. Various-sized rectangular windows were placed on each side, which framed breathtaking views of the East Branch of the AuSable River surrounded by the Adirondack Mountains. One purpose of the structure was to allow transport of iron ore from the Palmer Hill mines to mines and forges on the opposite side of the bridge (Wells 1996, 3). On June 12, 1997, the Jay Covered Bridge was dismantled, removed from across the river, and placed on land in a nearby park (Wilson 1997, 2). A new bridge will be built 400 feet downstream (Jeffrey 2000, 9). Once the new bridge is in operation, the old bridge will be placed back at its original site and serve as a pedestrian and bicycle crossing only. Reconstruction on the Jay Covered Bridge will probably start in 2003.

Salisbury Center Covered Bridge measures fifty feet in length and is the only remaining covered bridge in Herkimer County (south of the Adirondacks). The bridge was constructed in 1875 by Alvah Hopson at a cost of $478 (Michielsen and Michielsen 1998, 3). The Multiple Kingpost and Arch truss design is the only one of its type remaining of the New York State historic covered bridges. The bridge now rests on steel beams hidden under the floor (Wilson 1976, 5). Salisbury Covered Bridge Days became an annual event on June 6, 1998. Bridge ceremonies, a Civil War encampment, a fishing derby, a craft show, an exhibit of old tools, a chicken barbecue, a pancake breakfast, fast food, a play, a dance, fireworks, and a parade through the bridge were all part of the event (Michielsen and Michielsen 1998, 3).

Otsego County (central Leatherstocking) can claim the oldest covered bridge in New York State. Hyde Hall Covered Bridge, built in 1823, is the third-oldest existing covered bridge in North America according to the *World Guide to Covered Bridges* (1989). The bridge is still in its original location inside Glimmerglass State Park, spans fifty-three feet utilizing the Burr truss design, and is now limited to pedestrian traffic. George Hyde Clarke inherited the property from his great-grandfather, Lieutenant Governor George Clarke (*Glimmerglass State Park, n.d.*). *Glimmerglass* was home to several Leatherstocking Tales by James Fenimore Cooper, a series of five popular novels about American frontier life, most notably *The Last of the Mohicans* (Cooper 1995).

Copeland Covered Bridge, built by Arad Copeland in 1879, is the only historic covered bridge remaining in Saratoga County (south of the Adirondacks). Mr. Copeland, a farmer, constructed this bridge to move cattle from one side of Beecher Creek to the other. He used a Queenpost truss design that still spans thirty-five feet over Beecher Creek. This covered bridge has the only "true," not a truss combination, Queenpost truss design remaining in New York State. Picturesque Beecher Falls can be viewed from the bridge looking upstream. Copeland Covered Bridge is privately owned by the Edinburg Historical Society.

Schoharie County (north of the Catskills) is famous for an extremely rare covered bridge. Blenheim Covered Bridge is one of only six covered bridges with two lanes, or "double barrels," in the United States. It is the longest single-span (228 feet, and 210 feet clear-span) covered bridge in the world. This covered bridge is one of only three to be named a National Civil Engineering Landmark. The bridge is constructed with a Long and Center Arch truss design. The exterior wood is painted and stained a dark-brown color and the metal roof is painted a light-green color. The covered bridge has a fence across the west portal, but pedestrians may enter through the east portal. There is a picnic area with ample parking on the east bank of Shoharie Creek near the bridge. Nicholas Montgomery Powers from Pittsford, Vermont, was the builder of the Blenheim Covered Bridge in 1855. In laying the bridge out first on land, it was never made level but had a very slight arch or camber to it. This was to take care of any sag when its weight "set it to place." The amount of camber used was one of the builder's skills, for only he could take into consideration his inaccuracies along with the softness or shrinkage of the wood. The builder had to estimate exactly how much differential there would be when the structure was on its own. Powers said, "If the bridge goes down when we knock the trestle out from under it, I never want to see the sun rise again." To prove it, he sat in the middle with his legs dangling when the last chocks were knocked free. It sagged only a fraction of an inch, exactly to where he had predicted. They say that when an ardent prohibitionist town official came to inspect the bridge building, a jug of whiskey was hidden in the stone abutments, as the builder said, "like an alcoholic cornerstone" (Sloane 1954, 102–4).

Sullivan County (central Catskills) has four historic covered bridges remaining. Halls Mills Covered Bridge, built in 1912 by David Benton and John Knight, is the youngest of all twenty-four historic covered bridges. It is the longest in Sullivan County at 130 feet and uses Town Lattice trusses. This Catskill truss design does not utilize radiating braces at the vertical endposts but does have flying buttresses, and also has a Catskill-style wood approach ramp connected to the north abutment. The bridge was bypassed in 1962 and is now limited to pedestrian traffic, with a parking area nearby. The bridge is a perfect target for vandals, being off the beaten path, and has been used frequently by graffiti artists. A gauging station is within downstream view of the bridge.

Beaverkill Covered Bridge is an entranceway to Beaverkill State Park, a New York State Department of Environmental Conservation campground. This bridge is also a Town Lattice truss design and has a single-span of ninety-eight feet. John Davidson, a famous covered bridge builder in the Catskills, built this bridge in 1865. The structure is built on dry laid stone abutments. The west abutment has been resurfaced with concrete and now hides the stone. A wooden approach ramp is connected to the east abutment. The bridge has flying buttresses and radiating braces at the vertical endposts of the trusses. The park offers a deep, clear swimming hole and beach area, free public parking, fishing access, restroom facilities, changing rooms, and picnic areas (Bivins 1999, 8).

Van Tran Flat Covered Bridge is another Town Lattice truss design, measures 117 feet in length, and was built by John Davidson in 1860. This bridge has radiating braces at the vertical endposts of the trusses, flying buttresses, and a wooden approach ramp connected to the south abutment. It was closed in 1973 and reopened in 1985 after extensive repairs (Wilson 1991a, 15). Along with the authentic restoration, twenty plank laminated arches were installed under the technical assistance of Milton S. Graton, a noted covered bridge consultant from New Hampshire. The site offers free public parking areas, restroom facilities, fishing access, and picnic areas (Bivins 1999, 8).

At forty-eight feet, the fourth and smallest historic covered bridge in Sullivan County is the Bendo Covered Bridge, another Town Lattice truss design. Built by John Davidson in Livingston Manor in 1860, it was cut in half in 1913 and moved upstream by Joseph Sherwood to its current location at Covered Bridge Campsites. Radiating braces are only at one end of the vertical endposts of the trusses since it was divided. Framework used as flying buttresses (sway bracing beyond) are also part of this design. After a flood in 1970, a new abutment was constructed and the bridge was set on two iron beams that are now hidden under the trusses (Wilson 1976, 5). The area offers fishing access, free public parking, and picnic areas, and the campground is open to the public with amenities that include a general store and children's playground (Bivins 1999, 8).

In Tompkins County (southeast Finger Lakes) the Newfield Covered Bridge is a single span of 115 feet in length across the West Branch of Cayuga Creek, the oldest covered bridge still carrying daily traffic in New York State. The bridge was originally built in 1853 at a cost of $800 and uses the Town Lattice truss design. The diamond-shaped windows are framed by the Lattice truss and the exterior is a freshly painted barn red. In 1972, Milton S. Graton rehabilitated the bridge with twenty-one plank laminated arches, and a new roof was put on to raise the clearance of the portals (Wilson 1991a, 15). The bridge underwent another restoration from 1997 to 1998 and was reopened to traffic. There is now a beautiful overlook area where one can view the bridge and creek, dedicated to Grant and Marie Musser, "Keepers of the Bridge," who were instrumental in both renovations.

Ulster County (eastern Catskills) claims five historic covered bridges, the longest being Perrine's Covered Bridge at 154 feet. Built in 1844, it is the second-oldest covered bridge in New York State and uses the Burr truss design. The bridge was rehabilitated from 1997 to 1998 and is now on a bypassed section of Route 213 and limited to pedestrian traffic. The structure can be seen by motorists from the New York Thruway, particularly at night. A solitary light on the south shore, upstream side, and six lights on the upper chord of the west truss illuminate Perrine's Covered Bridge. This bridge was the first to receive money from the New York State Covered Bridge Society (Wilson 1976, 5). There is a picnic area on the west bank of the Wallkill River near the structure.

The Forge Covered Bridge and the Tappan Covered Bridge span Dry Brook and have similar Kingpost truss designs built by Jerome Moot in 1906. The Forge Covered Bridge has a length of twenty-seven feet, the smallest of all twenty-four remaining historic covered bridges. The bridge is privately owned and can be viewed from Dry Brook Road. With the only "authentic" historic Kingpost truss design in New York State and flying buttresses to prevent leaning or twisting, the bridge rests on stone abutments, which rest on stone ledges. Dry Brook has cut a narrow gorge through rock creating a scenic, not-to-be-missed setting downstream from the bridge.

Tappan Covered Bridge is also relatively small, measuring forty-three feet in length. Typical Catskill-style flying buttresses are part of the design. This bridge once had a noticeable sag and was held up by a cable attached to trees on opposite sides. The additional support given by steel girders, put underneath the bridge, has prolonged the bridge's daily use. Only the framing is part of the old structure built in 1906.

Ashokan/Turnwood Covered Bridge was built in 1885 by Nelson Tompkins over the Beaverkill River in Turnwood, N.Y. The hamlet was named after two small mills that specialized in making chair legs and wooden scoops. Due to heavy automobile traffic, the bridge was in dire need of repairs and declared unsafe by the town in June 1934. In 1938, a new steel highway bridge was built downstream from the covered bridge. Lester A. Moerhing, comptroller of the Chrysler Corporation, won the bridge with a bid of one dollar and moved it to his property over Esopus Creek in Olive, N.Y. After Mr. Moerhing died, Mrs. Moerhing sold the property, including the bridge, to Mr. and Mrs. Frank V. Banks in 1955. The State University of New Paltz bought the bridge and the land from the Banks in 1957 and called the area the Ashokan Campus (Miller n.d., 28, 30–31). The bridge is constructed with Town Lattice trusses, measures sixty-two feet in length, and has a pair of Catskill-style flying buttresses on each side. Mid-height windows were most likely added during the 1920s (Miller n.d., 28). Scenic Winchell Falls can be seen from the bridge.

Grants Mills Covered Bridge has a total length of sixty-six feet and was originally built in 1902 at a cost of $1027.97 and 203 construction man-days (Munson 1992, 6). The Town Lattice truss design has a single rectangular window framed between the trusswork on the north side. The bridge was bypassed in 1964 and is now open to pedestrian traffic only (Wilson 1991a, 16). The great-grandson of one of the original builders restored the bridge at a cost of approximately $13,000 and 149 construction man-days. Included in the cost of the renovation were two hundred new oak trunnels, at four dollars each, with donor names placed on them (Munson 1992, 6). The original trunnels were made from birch logs (Munson 1992, 4).

Washington County (northeast of Albany near the Vermont border) claims four historic covered bridges. Eagleville Covered Bridge is a Town Lattice truss design with a length of 101 feet. Constructed in 1858, it has been given new paint, sides, and shingles several times, and now has light-brown paint on the sides and white paint on the portals. Anglers often removed sideboards to fish the Battenkill River. To prevent further damage, a hinged door was built into the side of the bridge to allow fishing access. Some people endangered canoeists by jumping through this opening. A chain link fence is now in place along the entire length of the trusses to solve this problem (Wilson 1999). The bridge closed for repairs in 1998 and reopened in 1999. It has become a favorite location for swimming, picnicking, and fishing.

The Shushan Covered Bridge is now a private, nonprofit museum. Also built in 1858, it is a 161-foot-long double-span bridge with diamond-shaped windows framed by the Town Lattice truss. The Stevens brothers built the bridge, and folklore has it that on completion one of them exuberantly leaped off the newly shingled roof into the Battenkill River, fully clothed and waving his straw hat. Another story has the whole bridge-building crew taking an impromptu bath to celebrate their achievement. Before World War II, a facelift gave the bridge a modern appearance. New concrete abutments to replace the marble, a concrete center pier, a new roof, a coat of Venetian red paint, and white portals for better visibility were added improvements. The old painted letters below the date of construction were restored, complete with the original misspelled words:

Five dollars fine for rideing or driveing on this bridge faster than a walk

In 1963, the covered bridge was moved over a few feet and put on a new foundation to make way for a high-level highway bridge built just to the south (Allen 1991, 4). Although the covered bridge posted a safe load of five tons when bypassed, estimates showed that it could have continued to carry six times that amount without trouble. The Shushan Covered Bridge Museum was opened in 1975. It was born with the idea that the old bridge, itself the main attraction, would house an everchanging display of pieces on loan from all over the rural region. There are several old farms in Washington County that have supplied agricultural implements, tools, and domestic utensils from an earlier time that may be of interest to museum visitors of all ages. Many pieces have been donated to the museum, but most of what is displayed is on loan. The museum directors feel that the items should be put in working order whenever possible and demonstrated rather than merely displayed. This is done on Harvest Days in August of each year (Shushan Covered Bridge Museum, n.d.)

Rexleigh Covered Bridge is a 107-foot span Howe truss design. Built in 1874, this truss design appears to use the timber and iron tie-rod designs developed in 1840 by William Howe from Spencer, Massachusetts. Particularly unique are the seventy-pound cast-iron "shoes" that were used to fit the timbers into the joining ends of the iron rods. Also called pillow blocks, these iron joints were patented on February 10, 1857, by Reuben Comins of Troy, New York. The patentee's name and patent date appear on the old castings. White marble, cut and hauled from Baxter's nearby quarry, was used to build the abutments (Allen 1991, 4). Remarkably, the original slate roof survived more than one hundred years of heavy snow and flood waters before engineers determined that the loading from the slate itself was unsafe. From 1983 to 1984, Milton S. Graton took on the job of a full restoration and the roof was replaced with shakes (Allen 1991, 4). The exterior paint, side door, and chain link fence resembles that of the Eagleville Covered Bridge in Washington County.

Buskirk Covered Bridge spans 164 feet across the Hoosic River, the border between Rensselaer and Washington Counties. The bridge carries Rensselaer County Route 59 and Washington County Route 103. This structure is painted barn red with white trim, has Howe trusses, and is the only remaining New York State historic covered bridge that has windows with awnings. Thought to be between 1850 and 1880, the exact date of construction was uncertain to historians for many years. As it turns out, the Buskirk Covered Bridge was built before the Civil War in the summer of 1857 at a cost of $1500. The towns of Cambridge and Hoosic split the cost equally (Raymond 1995, 8). A sign near the north portal states that Buskirk Covered Bridge replaced a previous bridge built in 1804 and that this crossing served the Great Northern Turnpike beginning in 1799.

One might wonder what it would cost to build a covered bridge today compared to the original cost. Robert W. Raymond, a Cambridge Village historian, and his colleague Dave Thornton had often pondered the relative value of "then-year" and current dollars. When someone tells a tale about the old days and a money figure is mentioned, it is invariably followed by the obligatory phrase, "and that was a lot of money in those days." But they do not bother translating the figure into today's amount. Covered bridges built before the Civil War (1861–65) had currency rates that were relatively stable. The silver-to-gold exchange rate was sixteen-to-one, and inflation since the Great Depression is around twenty times. Raymond and Thornton used sixteen times twenty, or 320, to multiply "then-year" dollars to get today's cost. Therefore, the Buskirk Covered Bridge would cost $1500 x 320 to build, or approximately $480,000 in today's dollars (Raymond 1995, 8).

In recent years, as the old bridges begin to disappear from the scene, interest in them has increased. Enthusiasts have organized groups devoted to covered bridge lore. One such group is the New York State Covered Bridge Society, formed in 1966 to bring enthusiasts together to help preserve the historic spans.

Other purposes of the society are to work with local communities interested in saving bridges, to collect information on all New York State covered bridges, and to make such historical information available to its members. The society year, which has eight meetings and one safari, begins in March and ends in November. Meetings are held in various locations, usually on the second Sunday of the month. Newsletters are sent to members, giving the location and directions to the meeting place. Also included in the newsletter is information received about bridges and a report of the business conducted at the meeting. *The Empire State Courier,* the official publication of the society, is published three times a year. The publication shares pictures and interesting stories about covered bridges. The information is about bridges that no longer exist, old covered spans that are in daily use, and those that are bypassed and still standing (*Covered Bridges in New York State,* n.d.).

Acknowledgments

SEVERAL FAMILY MEMBERS AND FRIENDS generously provided assistance in transforming this book into a reality. Most sincere gratitude and appreciation are reserved for the following people:

Lori Barron, my sister, for use of her computer in numerous hours of manuscript preparation.

Abby and Tyler Barron, my niece and nephew, for unselfishly sharing computer time.

Brad Berfield, my brother, for encouraging me to capture these beautiful "timber crossings" on film while gathering statistics.

Midge Berfield, my sister-in-law, for spending many tedious hours proofreading and rewriting my preface.

Wayne and June Berfield, my parents, for proposing the concept of a guide and encouraging me to submit my manuscript. Also, a special thank you to my mom for countless hours of typing and proofreading.

Richard T. Donovan, Vice President of the Theodore Burr Covered Bridge Society, Inc., for reviewing my manuscript in detail and correcting errors in text.

Richard Wilson, President of the New York State Covered Bridge Society, for the picturesque photography which enhances this book, for reviewing my manuscript in detail, and for correcting errors in the text and being the guide's architectural historian.

Special gratitude to the staff of Syracuse University Press for dedication, encouragement, and patience in guiding me through this publication.

Covered Bridges and Their Locations

Delaware County

1. Downsville
2. Fitch's
3. Hamden
4. Tuscarora Club (Demis)
5. Lower Shaverton (Campbell's)

Essex County

6. Jay

Herkimer County

7. Salisbury Center

Otsego County

8. Hyde Hall

Saratoga County

9. Copeland

Schoharie County

10. Blenheim

Sullivan County

11. Halls Mills
12. Beaverkill (Conklin)
13. Van Tran Flat
   (Livingston Manor)
14. Bendo

Tompkins County

15. Newfield

Ulster County

16. Perrine's
17. Forge
18. Tappen (Kittle)
19. Ashokan/Turnwood
   (New Paltz Campus, Olive)
20. Grants Mills

Washington County

21. Eagleville
22. Shushan
23. Rexleigh
24. Buskirk*

*Rensselaer and Washington Counties

How to Use This Book As a Guide

THE COVERED BRIDGES IN THIS GUIDE are arranged numerically by respective "covered bridge assigned number." Each bridge is located on the state map, has at least one color photograph (except Tuscarora Club Covered Bridge), statistical information, field observation notes, and a truss diagram.

The map of New York State is intended to give the reader a feel for where the covered bridges are located.

There are twenty-four vivid color photographs. Hamden Covered Bridge is featured twice: before July 19, 2000, and after its restoration. The photographs were intended to capture some of the beauty of each covered bridge. However, to really experience and appreciate the true beauty of these timeless wooden crossings, one must visit them in person.

The directions are somewhat simple, but with a little effort and a good map, the bridges are easier to locate than one might realize. After all, the thrill of finding one of these rare gems is all part of the wonderful experience enthusiasts call bridging.

The statistical information includes the common name of the bridge followed by other known names. The municipality and county in which the bridge is located are below the bridge name. The statistical information is listed under a variety of headings. Below is an explanation of those headings:

YEAR BUILT: The original date the bridge was constructed.

TRUSS SYSTEM: The framework of timbers only or timbers and bars that support each other and remain rigid (See individual truss diagrams).

ROADWAY CARRIED: The roadway that spans the waterway.

WATERWAY CROSSED: The river, creek, or brook that the roadway crosses.

WEIGHT LIMIT: The bridge is either closed, has a weight limit sign (posted), or has an unknown weight limit.

NUMBER OF SPANS: The number of observed spans.

LENGTH: The length from portal to portal measured in feet at the floor line.

CLEAR WIDTH: The minimum width of the approach or bridge opening measured in feet and inches.

OUT-TO-OUT WIDTH: The maximum width of the bridge measured in feet and inches (excluding flying buttresses).

CLEARANCE: The minimum vertical clearance at the portals is either measured in feet and inches or has a clearance sign (posted).

BUILDER(S): The original contractor(s) who built the bridge.

OWNERSHIP: The bridge has either state, county, township, or private ownership.

COVERED BRIDGE ASSIGNED NUMBER: The first two letters represent the state. The next two digits represent the county, assigned alphabetically. The last two digits represent a specific bridge within the county, assigned in the order data was received by the WGCB (World Guide to Covered Bridges) compilers.

∎ ∎ ∎

The field observation notes are also listed under a variety of headings. Below is a series of questions I asked myself while observing these bridges in the field:

SIDES:

What type of wood siding is on the exterior sides of the bridge?

What color is the wood siding?

Is there an opening underneath the eaves?

How many flying buttresses (lateral exterior supports) are there? How many are there on each side? Approximately how high are they? What type of material covers them? Are they made from framework?

How many ledges are there? How many are there on each side? Approximately how high are they? Approximately how long are they?

PORTALS:

What type of wood siding is on the exterior portals of the bridge?

What color is the wood siding?

Are they made from framework?

What color is the trim painted?

What type of overhang does the roof make with the sides, looking from the side?

What is the shape of the bottom of the gable (triangular section enclosed by sloping ends of roof)?

FLOORING:

Is there tire track planking laid over deck planking? If so, which direction does the tire track planking face?

Which direction does the deck planking face?

ROOF:

What type of material covers the roof?

Does the roof have a metal ridge cap?

ABUTMENTS:

What materials were used to construct the abutments?

WINGWALLS:

What materials were used to construct the wingwalls?

PIERS:

How many piers support the bridge?

What type of a pier supports the bridge?

WINDOWS:

How many windows are there?

Where are the windows located?

What are the shapes of the windows?

Do the windows have awnings?

DOORS:

How many doors are there?

Where are the doors located?

SKEW ANGLE:

What is the angle from side to side, looking down on the structure?

Is there any other relevant information about the bridge?

Are there any informational signs on the bridge? What do they say and where are they located?

Are there any informational signs near the bridge? What do they say?

Are there any informational monuments near the bridge? What do they say?

Solid truss lines represent wooden members and dashed truss lines represent iron tie rods.

At the end of this guide is a mileage table. The table shows approximate driving distances between towns where (or near which) the covered bridges are located. Also, at the end of this guide are quick reference lists for year built, length, National Register of Historic Places, clearance, and weight limit. The latter two lists apply to covered bridges in daily use only.

Covered Bridges *of* New York State

Downsville

Colchester, Delaware County

LOCATION: Bridge Street, 0.1 mile off Route 30 at the east end of the village of Downsville.

YEAR BUILT: 1854

TRUSS SYSTEM: Long with Queenpost

ROADWAY CARRIED: Bridge Street

WATERWAY CROSSED: East Branch Delaware River

WEIGHT LIMIT: 3 tons

NUMBER OF SPANS: 1

LENGTH: 174'

CLEAR WIDTH: 8'-1" (guide rail to guide rail)

OUT-TO-OUT WIDTH: 18'-10"

CLEARANCE: 6'-0"

BUILDER: Robert Murray

OWNERSHIP: County

COVERED BRIDGE ASSIGNED NUMBER: NY-13–01

Field Observations

SIDES: Nonuniform and vertical siding
    Color: Natural wood
    Opening under eaves: Yes
    Flying buttresses: 8
        Location: 4 per side
        Height: One-quarter of the way up from
            bottom
        End caps: Natural wood
    Ledges: None
PORTALS: Nonuniform and vertical siding
    Color: Natural wood
    Trim: None
    Overhang: Inward sloping from top
    Gables: Horizontal
FLOORING: Tire-track planking: None
    Deck planking: Lengthwise (middle two-thirds is
        treated)
ROOF: Shakes
ABUTMENTS: Concrete
WINGWALLS: NE: Concrete
PIERS: None
WINDOWS: None
DOORS: None
SKEW ANGLE: 0 degrees

■ ■ ■

Black stenciled signs on truss systems:

Free Illustrated Booklet
"Covered Bridges"
Write
Covered Bridge Heritage
Box 12 Jenkintown, PA 19046

Note: The author wrote for this booklet, but address was unknown.

■ ■ ■

Yellow and blue New York State sign:

Downsville Covered Bridge
Built in 1854 by Robert Murray to span 174'
of the east branch at a cost of $1,700.
Restored in 1998 for $1,000,000 as a tribute
to the skills of the past.
    Donated by Downsville Women's Club

Fitch's

Delhi, Delaware County

Original Bridge

LOCATION: From Delhi, take Route 10 northeast for 3.5 miles. The bridge will be on the right and you can see it from the highway.

YEAR BUILT: 1870

TRUSS SYSTEM: Town

ROADWAY CARRIED: Fitch's Bridge Road

WATERWAY CROSSED: West Branch Delaware River

WEIGHT LIMIT: 3 tons

NUMBER OF SPANS: 1

LENGTH: 100'

CLEAR WIDTH: 14'-0"

OUT-TO-OUT WIDTH: 19'-10"

CLEARANCE: 9'-0"

BUILDERS: James Frazier and James Warren

OWNERSHIP: County

COVERED BRIDGE ASSIGNED NUMBER: NY-13–02

Field Observations

SIDES: Nonuniform and vertical siding
    Color: Barn red paint
    Opening under eaves: Yes
    Flying buttresses: 8
      Location: 4 per side
      Height: Full
      End caps: Barn red wood
    Ledges: None
PORTALS: Nonuniform and vertical siding
    Color: Barn red paint
    Trim: None
    Overhang: 90 degrees
    Gables: Chamfered

FLOORING: Tire-track planking: None
    Deck planking: Crosswise
ROOF: Metal
ABUTMENTS: North: Concrete
    South: Stone
WINGWALLS: NW: Sheet piling
    NE: Stone on top of concrete
    SW & SE: Stone
PIERS: None
WINDOWS: None
DOORS: None
SKEW ANGLE: 0 degrees

■ ■ ■

This covered bridge has inside weatherboards.

Hamden

Hamden, Delaware County

Original Bridge

Statistics and field observations based on conditions before July 19, 2000.

LOCATION: The bridge can be seen from Route 10 at the east end of the village of Hamden on the right while going northeast. This bridge was accidentally dropped into the river on July 19, 2000, while being dismantled, but is now completely restored.

YEAR BUILT: 1859
TRUSS SYSTEM: Long

ROADWAY CARRIED: Basin Clove Road
WATERWAY CROSSED: West Branch Delaware River
WEIGHT LIMIT: 3 tons

NUMBER OF SPANS: Built as a single-span bridge; pier installed in the 1940s.

LENGTH: 125'

CLEAR WIDTH: 8'-6" (guide rail to guide rail)

OUT-TO-OUT WIDTH: 18'-6"

CLEARANCE: 6'-0"

BUILDER: Robert Murray

OWNERSHIP: County

COVERED BRIDGE ASSIGNED NUMBER: NY-13–03

Field Observations

SIDES: Nonuniform and vertical siding

  Color: Natural wood/faded barn red paint

  Opening under eaves: Yes

  Flying buttresses: 8

   Location: 4 per side

   Height:

    Ends: One-third of the way up from bottom

    Intermediates: Full

   End caps: Metal

  Ledges: None

PORTALS: Nonuniform and vertical siding

  Color: Natural wood/faded barn red paint

  Trim: None

  Overhang: 90 degrees

  Gables:

   North: Chamfered

   South: Horizontal

FLOORING: Tire-track planking: None

  Deck planking: Crosswise

ROOF: Metal

ABUTMENTS: Concrete caps on top of stone with concrete footings

WINGWALLS: Stone

PIERS: 1

  Type: Wood trestle

WINDOWS: 4

  Location: 2 per side

  Shape: Rectangular

  Awnings: None

DOORS: None

SKEW ANGLE: 0 degrees

■ ■ ■

Black stenciled signs on truss systems (see p. 3).
White letters on south portal:

Hamden Covered Bridge

Year Built: 1859

Cost: $1000

Builder: Robert Murray

Length: 128' single span

Type: Long's panel truss

This bridge replaced an open deck flat bridge which stood at the same location. Prior to that, some fifty rods upstream, a bridge using bents and poles carried the Kingston Turnpike travelers across the West Branch of the Delaware River.

Restored Bridge

Field observations based on conditions on August 27, 2001.

TRUSS SYSTEM: Long

ROADWAY CARRIED: Basin Clove Road

WATERWAY CROSSED: West Branch Delaware River

WEIGHT LIMIT: 3 tons

NUMBER OF SPANS: 1

LENGTH: 130'

CLEAR WIDTH: 8'-7" (guide rail to guide rail)

OUT-TO-OUT WIDTH: 18'-7"

CLEARANCE: 9'-0"

BUILDER: Robert Murray

OWNERSHIP: County

COVERED BRIDGE ASSIGNED NUMBER: NY-13–03

Field Observations

SIDES: Uniform and vertical siding
    Color: Natural wood
    Opening under eaves: Yes
    Flying buttresses: None
    Ledges: None
PORTALS: Uniform and vertical siding
    Color: Natural wood

Trim: None
    Overhang: 90 degrees
    Gables: Chamfered
FLOORING: Tire-track planking: None
    Deck planking: Lengthwise
ROOF: Metal
ABUTMENTS: Concrete caps on top of stone with
                concrete footings
WINGWALLS: Stone
PIERS: None
WINDOWS: 4
    Location: 2 per side
    Shape: Rectangular
    Awnings: None
DOORS: None
SKEW ANGLE: 0 degrees

■   ■   ■

A park is proposed to be built on the southwest side of the covered bridge.

Black stenciled signs on truss systems (see p. 3).
White letters on south portal:

Hamden Covered Bridge
Year Built: 1859
Cost: $1000
Builder: Robert Murray
Length: 128' single span
Type: Long's panel truss

This bridge replaced an open deck flat bridge which stood at the same location. Prior to that, some fifty rods upstream, a bridge using bents and poles carried the Kingston Turnpike travelers across the West Branch of the Delaware River.

Front side of yellow and blue New York State sign:

Hamden Covered Bridge
Built in 1859 by Robert Murray to Span 128' of the west branch at a cost of $1,000. Restored in 2000 for $558,000 by W. L. Kline, Inc., as a tribute to the skills of the past. This plaque donated by descendants of Robert Murray.

Reverse side of yellow and blue New York State sign:

Hamden Covered Bridge
Built in 1859 and placed on the State and National Registers of Historic Places in 1999. This plaque donated by the town of Hamden.

Tuscarora Club (Demis)

Middletown, Delaware County

LOCATION: Not available. The members of the Tuscarora Club do not wish to have visitors.

YEAR BUILT: 1870

TRUSS SYSTEM: Formerly Kingpost, now Stringer.

ROADWAY CARRIED: Private

WATERWAY CROSSED: Mill Brook

WEIGHT LIMIT: Closed

NUMBER OF SPANS: 1

LENGTH: 38'

CLEAR WIDTH: 12'-10"

OUT-TO-OUT WIDTH: 14'-6"

CLEARANCE: 9'-0"

BUILDER: William Mead

OWNERSHIP: Private

COVERED BRIDGE ASSIGNED NUMBER: NY-13–05

Field Observations

SIDES: Nonuniform and horizontal shake siding
    Color: Natural wood
    Opening under eaves: No
    Flying buttresses: 6
        Location: 3 per side

Height: Full
    End Caps: Shakes
    Ledges: None

PORTALS: Nonuniform and horizontal shake siding
    Color: Natural wood
    Trim: None
    Overhang: Inward sloping from top (upper quarter)
        Vertical (lower three-quarters)
    Gables: Horizontal

FLOORING: Tire-track planking: None
    Deck planking: Crosswise

ROOF: Wooden shingles

ABUTMENTS: Stone and mortar

WINGWALLS: SE & SW: Stone and mortar

PIERS: None

WINDOWS: 2
    Location: 1 per side
    Shape: Trapezoidal
    Awnings: None

DOORS: None

SKEW ANGLE: 0 degrees

■ ■ ■

Bench against north truss.

Stone and mortar steps leading down from west portal.

Lower Shavertown (Campbell's)

Hancock, Delaware County

LOCATION: From Roscoe, take County Route 96 to the north end of Tennanah Lake. Turn right on the road to Lake Muskoday. In three miles, on your right, is the bridge. Permission is needed to view this private bridge.

YEAR BUILT: 1877

TRUSS SYSTEM: Town

ROADWAY CARRIED: Private

WATERWAY CROSSED: Trout Brook

WEIGHT LIMIT: Unknown

NUMBER OF SPANS: 1

LENGTH: 32'

CLEAR WIDTH: 12'-11"

OUT-TO-OUT WIDTH: 16'-3"

CLEARANCE: 11'-6"

BUILDERS: Anson Jenkins and August Neidig

OWNERSHIP: Private

COVERED BRIDGE ASSIGNED NUMBER: NY-13–07

Field Observations

SIDES: Uniform and vertical siding

    Color: Natural wood

    Opening under eaves: Yes

    Flying buttresses: 4

      Location: 2 per side

      Height: Full

      End caps: Natural wood

    Ledges: None

PORTALS: Uniform and vertical siding on gables

    Nonuniform and vertical siding on uprights

    Color: Natural wood

    Trim: None

    Overhang: Inward sloping from top (upper half)

     Vertical (lower half)

    Gables: Square

FLOORING: Tire-track planking: Lengthwise

    Deck planking: Crosswise

ROOF: Shakes

ABUTMENTS: Stone

WINGWALLS: NE, NW & SW: Stone

PIERS: None

WINDOWS: None

DOORS: None

SKEW ANGLE: 0 degrees

■ ■ ■

Black stenciled signs on truss system (see p. 3):

    License plates, horseshoes, and old tools attached to roof supports and trusses.

    Old advertisements also posted to roof supports and trusses.

    Milk cans located near west portal uprights. Hitching post located near right upright of west portal.

■ ■ ■

White and black sign at mid-height south inside (west end):

In Loving Memory of June Mary McMichael

June 1, 1945–May 14, 1997

God saw you getting tired and a cure was not to be.

So He put His arms around you and whispered "come to me."

Although we loved you dearly, we couldn't make you stay.

A precious heart stopped beating, hard working hands at rest.

God broke our hearts to prove us, He only takes the best.

If it only took our love to keep you with us, you would have lived forever.

    "In our hearts forever!"

Love,

Bill, Laurie, Bill Jr., Shawn

Black and yellow sign on left upright of west portal:

Horse Drawn Vehicles

Jay

Jay, Essex County

Statistics and field observations based on conditions before June 12, 1997.

LOCATION: In Jay, turn east at the park. A sign points the way. On June 12, 1997, this covered bridge was dismantled, removed from across the river, and placed in a nearby park. A temporary roadway bridge spans the existing piers.

YEAR BUILT: 1857
TRUSS SYSTEM: Howe

ROADWAY CARRIED: County Route 22 (Glen Road)
WATERWAY CROSSED: East Branch AuSable River

WEIGHT LIMIT: 3 tons

NUMBER OF SPANS: Built as a single-span bridge; four piers installed in the 1950s.

LENGTH: 175'

CLEAR WIDTH: 15'-7"

OUT-TO-OUT WIDTH: 20'-9"

CLEARANCE: 8'-0"

BUILDER: George M. Burt

OWNERSHIP: County

COVERED BRIDGE ASSIGNED NUMBER: NY-16–01

Field Observations

SIDES: Uniform and vertical siding
    Color: Natural wood
    Opening under eaves: No
    Flying buttresses: None
    Ledges: None

PORTALS: Uniform and vertical siding
    Color: Faded light-brown paint
    Trim: None
    Overhang: 90 degrees
    Gables: Horizontal

FLOORING: Tire-track planking: Not available
    Deck planking: Not available

ROOF: Shakes

ABUTMENTS: East: Stone and mortar
    West: Concrete

WINGWALLS: NE & SE: Stone and mortar
    NW & SW: Concrete

PIERS: 4
    Type: 3 steel columns anchored in concrete
        footings

WINDOWS: Not available

DOORS: None

SKEW ANGLE: 0 degrees

■   ■   ■

This bridge is posted with "No Trespassing" signs.
Wreath is on existing south gable.
Flower boxes are on uprights of existing south portal.

Black and white sign on both gables:

Built 1857

Salisbury Center

Salisbury Center, Herkimer County

LOCATION: Turn off State Route 29 and State Route 29A onto Water Street. Signs mark the way.

YEAR BUILT: 1875

TRUSS SYSTEM: Multiple Kingpost and Arch

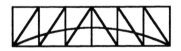

ROADWAY CARRIED: Fairview Road

WATERWAY CROSSED: Spruce Creek

WEIGHT LIMIT: 3 tons

NUMBER OF SPANS: 1

LENGTH: 50'

CLEAR WIDTH: 13'-3"

OUT-TO-OUT WIDTH: 15'-4"

CLEARANCE: 7'-6"

BUILDER: Alvah Hopson

OWNERSHIP: Township

COVERED BRIDGE ASSIGNED NUMBER: NY-22–01

Field Observations

SIDES: Uniform and vertical siding

    Color: Natural wood

    Opening under eaves: Yes

    Flying buttresses: None

    Ledges: None

PORTALS: Framework both portals

    Color: Natural wood

    Trim: None

    Overhang: 90 degrees

    Gables: Open

FLOORING: Tire-track planking: Lengthwise

    Deck planking: Crosswise

ROOF: Metal

ABUTMENTS: Concrete

WINGWALLS: Stone and mortar

PIERS: None

WINDOWS: None

DOORS: None

SKEW ANGLE: 0 degrees

■ ■ ■

Black and white signs on framework across both portals:

One dollar fine for crossing this Bridge faster than a Walk.

Concrete Monument:

Covered Bridge
Erected in 1875 by Alvah Hopson
Spruce Creek—at one time furnished waterpower
for nine nearby mills
This bridge is preserved by:
The Salisbury Town Board
The Salisbury Historical Society
The New York State Covered Bridge Society
The Bridge is on the
National Register of Historic Sites
Plaque—1979

Hyde Hall

Glimmerglass State Park, Otsego County

LOCATION: From East Springfield on State Route 20, go south on County Route 31 to Glimmerglass State Park. The bridge is on the right about a quarter of a mile from the entrance.

YEAR BUILT: 1823

TRUSS SYSTEM: Burr

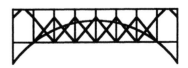

ROADWAY CARRIED: East Lake Road

WATERWAY CROSSED: Shadow Brook

WEIGHT LIMIT: Closed

NUMBER OF SPANS: 1

LENGTH: 53'

CLEAR WIDTH: 13'-4"

OUT-TO-OUT WIDTH: 15'-9"

CLEARANCE: 9'-0"

BUILDERS: Cyrenus Clark (master carpenter), Andrew Alden (local carpenter), and Lorenzo Bates (mason)

OWNERSHIP: State (admission)

COVERED BRIDGE ASSIGNED NUMBER: NY-39–01

Field Observations

SIDES: Uniform and horizontal siding

    Color: Natural wood

    Opening under eaves: No

    Flying buttresses: None

    Ledges: None

PORTALS: Uniform and horizontal siding on gables

    Uniform and vertical siding on uprights

Color: Natural wood

Trim: None

Overhang: 90 degrees

Gables: Rounded

FLOORING: Tire-track planking: None

    Deck planking: Lengthwise

ROOF: Wooden shingles

ABUTMENTS: Stone and mortar

WINGWALLS: Stone and mortar

PIERS: None

WINDOWS: None

DOORS: None

SKEW ANGLE: 0 degrees

. . .

This is the oldest covered bridge in New York State.

Lower 3' of Burr Arch is protected by wood, and the remainder is covered by a chain link fence.

Copeland

Edinburg, Saratoga County

LOCATION: Edinburg is located near the large bridge across the Great Sacandaga Lake at Batchellerville. In Edinburg, take County Route 4 (North Shore Road) north for a half-mile to the bridge. Permission is needed to view this private bridge.

YEAR BUILT: 1879

TRUSS SYSTEM: Queenpost

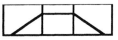

ROADWAY CARRIED: Private

WATERWAY CROSSED: Beecher Creek

WEIGHT LIMIT: Closed

NUMBER OF SPANS: 1

LENGTH: 35'
CLEAR WIDTH: 8'-7"
OUT-TO-OUT WIDTH: 11'-7"
CLEARANCE: 6'-10"
BUILDER: Arad Copeland
OWNERSHIP: Private
COVERED BRIDGE ASSIGNED NUMBER: NY-46–01

Field Observations

SIDES: Nonuniform and vertical siding
    Color: Natural wood
    Opening under eaves: No
    Flying buttresses: None
    Ledges: None
PORTALS: Nonuniform and vertical siding
    Color: Natural wood
    Trim: None
    Overhang: 90 degrees
    Gables: Chamfered
FLOORING: Tire-track planking: None
    Deck planking: Crosswise
ROOF: Metal
ABUTMENTS: Stone
WINGWALLS: Stone
PIERS: None
WINDOWS: 2
    Location: 1 per side
    Shape: Rectangular
    Awnings: None
DOORS: None
SKEW ANGLE: 0 degrees

■ ■ ■

Crisscross picket fences at north portal. However, you may enter covered bridge with permission.

Yellow letters on north gable:

Arad Copeland 1879
Maximum load 10 adults

Red, black, and white sign:

No Trespassing
Property of Edinburg Historical Society

Black and white sign:

The project is funded by the *Rural New York Grant Program* administered by the Preservation League of New York State with the support of *The J. M. Kaplan Fund, the Andy Warhol Foundation for the Visual Arts, the Margaret L. Wrendt Foundation, Philip Morris Companies, Inc., Corning Incorporated Foundation, and the Northern New York Community Foundation, Inc.*

Yellow and blue Saratoga County sign:

Saratoga County 2000
Covered bridge built by Arad Copeland below Beecher Falls in 1879. Only NYS Queenpost truss bridge. Placed on NYS and National Register in 1998.
Erected by Town of Edinburg.

Blenheim

Blenheim, Schoharie County

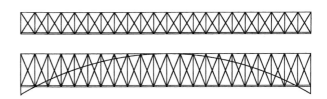

LOCATION: The bridge is just off State Route 30 at the north end of North Blenheim.

YEAR BUILT: 1855

TRUSS SYSTEM: Long and Center Arch

ROADWAY CARRIED: Bypassed section of Route 30

WATERWAY CROSSED: Schoharie Creek

WEIGHT LIMIT: Closed
NUMBER OF SPANS: 1
LENGTH: 228'
CLEAR WIDTH: 2 x 10'-2"
OUT-TO-OUT WIDTH: 27'-10"
CLEARANCE: 12'-6"
BUILDER: Nicholas Montgomery Powers
OWNERSHIP: County
COVERED BRIDGE ASSIGNED NUMBER: NY-48–01

Field Observations

SIDES: Uniform and vertical siding
    Color: Dark-brown paint
    Opening under eaves: Yes
    Flying buttresses: None
    Ledges: None
PORTALS: Uniform and vertical siding
    Color:
        Gables: Dark-brown stain
        Uprights: Dark-brown paint
    Trim: None
    Overhang: Outward sloping from top
    Gables:
        West: Square
        East: Triangular
FLOORING: Tire-track planking: None
    Deck planking: Lengthwise
ROOF: Metal
ABUTMENTS: West: Concrete, stone, and mortar
        with stone fill
    East: Stone and mortar on concrete with
        stone fill
WINGWALLS: SE: Stone and mortar on concrete

PIERS: None
WINDOWS: None
DOORS: None
SKEW ANGLE: 0 degrees

■ ■ ■

This is the longest single-span covered bridge in the world and only one of six bridges with two lanes in the United States.

There is a wood fence across the west portal.

Black and white sign at top of south truss (west end):

In the spring of 1869 a severe freshet washed out a wide channel across the western approach. A wooden extension was added to the Blenheim Bridge to span the new channel. In 1895 it was replaced by an iron extension. The wooden covered bridge was retired from use in 1931 and the board of supervisors voted to retain the bridge as a public historical relic.

Black and white sign on west gable:

Old covered bridge; longest single span wooden bridge of its type in the world; built 1855 232 ft long

Red, black, and white sign on east gable:

$5.00 fine to ride or drive this bridge faster than a walk

Yellow and blue New York State sign:

New York
Blenheim Bridge
Longest single span wooden bridge in world.
Built by Blenheim Bridge Company, Incorpo-
rated 1828. Last of its kind in this region.
State Education Department 1935

Concrete Monument:

National Historic Civil
Engineering Landmark
Blenheim Bridge

Concrete Monument:

Old Blenheim Bridge
Erected 1854–1855 by Nicholas
Montgomery Powers
Famous bridge builder
Born Pittsford, Vermont August 30, 1817
Died Clarendon, Vermont 1897

This bridge, 232 feet in length, the longest covered single-span wooden bridge in the world, was built for the Blenheim Bridge Company and was used as a toll bridge for many years. Not far from this bridge the Tory, William Beacraft, was whipped to death by his infuriated neighbors after the revolution. He was buried at the spot where he fell. The bridge is now under the custody of Schoharie County.
Erected by State Education Department and
Schoharie County Historical Society. 1935

Marble Monument:

Old Blenheim Bridge has been designated a registered national historic landmark under the provisions of the historic sites act of August 21, 1935. This site possesses exceptional value in commemorating and illustrating the history of the United States
U.S. Department of the Interior
National Park Service 1964

Halls Mills

Neversink, Sullivan County

LOCATION: From Curry, N.Y. on Route 55, go north on County Route 19 for almost three miles, turn left on Hunter Road for 0.3 mile, park, and take the abandoned road on the left to the bridge.

YEAR BUILT: 1912

TRUSS SYSTEM: Town

ROADWAY CARRIED: Bypassed section of Hunter Road

WATERWAY CROSSED: Neversink River

WEIGHT LIMIT: Closed

NUMBER OF SPANS: 1

LENGTH: 130'

CLEAR WIDTH: 13'-3"

OUT-TO-OUT WIDTH: 18'-3"

CLEARANCE: 8'-0"

BUILDERS: David Benton and John Knight

OWNERSHIP: County

COVERED BRIDGE ASSIGNED NUMBER: NY-53–01

Field Observations

SIDES: Nonuniform and vertical siding

    Color: Natural wood

    Opening under eaves: Yes

    Flying buttresses: 12

      Location: 6 per side

      Height: Full

      End caps: Metal

    Ledges: None

PORTALS: Uniform and vertical siding

    Color: Natural wood

    Trim: None

Overhang: Inward sloping from top

    Gables: Horizontal

FLOORING: Tire-track planking: Lengthwise

    Deck planking: Crosswise

ROOF: Metal

ABUTMENTS: North: Stone

    South: Stone on top of concrete

WINGWALLS: SE & SW: Stone on top of concrete

PIERS: None

WINDOWS: None

DOORS: None

SKEW ANGLE: 0 degrees

■   ■   ■

Approach ramp connected to north abutment.

Black stenciled signs on truss systems (see p. 3).

Beaverkill (Conklin)

Rockland, Sullivan County

LOCATION: From Livingston Manor, follow signs to Beaverkill State Park or go west on old Route 17 for about 1.5 miles, then go north on County Route 179 (Beaverkill Road) for five miles, then left on Beaverkill Camp Road for less than a mile to the bridge.

YEAR BUILT: 1865

TRUSS SYSTEM: Town

ROADWAY CARRIED: Campsite Road

WATERWAY CROSSED: Beaverkill Creek

WEIGHT LIMIT: 3 tons

NUMBER OF SPANS: 1

LENGTH: 98'

CLEAR WIDTH: 12'-10"

OUT-TO-OUT WIDTH: 16'-2"

CLEARANCE: 6'-6"

BUILDER: John Davidson

OWNERSHIP: County

COVERED BRIDGE ASSIGNED NUMBER: NY-53–02

Field Observations

SIDES: Uniform and vertical siding
    Color: Natural wood
    Opening under eaves: Yes
    Flying buttresses: 8
      Location: 4 per side
      Height: Full
      End caps: Metal
    Ledges: None
PORTALS: Nonuniform and vertical siding
    Color: Natural wood
    Trim: None
    Overhang: 90 degrees
    Gables: Chamfered
FLOORING: Tire-track planking: None
    Deck planking: Lengthwise
ROOF: Metal
ABUTMENTS: East: Concrete cap on top of stone
    West: Concrete
WINGWALLS: None
PIERS: None
WINDOWS: None
DOORS: None
SKEW ANGLE: 0 degrees

■ ■ ■

Approach ramp connected to east abutment.

Black stenciled signs on truss systems (see p. 3).
Yellow and blue New York State sign:

The Beaverkill Covered Bridge
Catskill State Preserve
Originally stone abutments
118 ft Towne lattice truss
Built by John Davidson
Erected by Town of Rockland

Yellow and blue New York State sign:

Covered Bridge Pool
This stretch of the Beaverkill was a favorite of
Theodore Gordon (1854–1915). Fly fisher,
fly-tier and creator of the Quill Gordon, one
of the first purely American dry flies.
Erected by Theodore Gordon Flyfishers

Van Tran Flat (Livingston Manor)

Rockland, Sullivan County

LOCATION: About one mile from Livingston Manor on old Route 17, turn left and go 0.3 mile to the bridge.

YEAR BUILT: 1860

TRUSS SYSTEM: Town and Laminated Arch

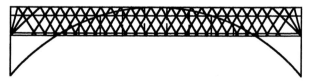

ROADWAY CARRIED: Covered Bridge Road

WATERWAY CROSSED: Willowemoc Creek

WEIGHT LIMIT: 5 tons

NUMBER OF SPANS: 1

LENGTH: 117'

CLEAR WIDTH: 11'-1" (arch-to-arch)

OUT-TO-OUT WIDTH: 16'-6"

CLEARANCE: 7'-8"

BUILDER: John Davidson

OWNERSHIP: County

COVERED BRIDGE ASSIGNED NUMBER: NY-53–03

Field Observations

SIDES: Uniform and vertical siding
    Color: Natural wood
    Opening under eaves: Yes
    Flying buttresses: 8
      Location: 4 per side
      Height: Full
      End caps: Shakes
    Ledges: None

PORTALS: Uniform and vertical siding
    Color: Natural wood
    Trim: None
    Overhang: 90 degrees
    Gables: Chamfered

FLOORING: Tire-track planking: None
    Deck planking: Lengthwise and crosswise

ROOF: Metal

ABUTMENTS: North: Stone faced with concrete
    South: Concrete

WINGWALLS: NE & NW: Concrete caps on top of
                stone

PIERS: None

WINDOWS: None

DOORS: None

SKEW ANGLE: 0 degrees

▪ ▪ ▪

Approach ramp connected to south abutment.

White and brown park sign:

Livingston Manor Covered Bridge
This bridge, originally known as the Mott's Flat Bridge and more recently the Vantran Flat Bridge, is one of several remaining Catskill type covered wooden bridges. Built by John Davidson in 1860, it is the oldest of four remaining in Sullivan County of the patented Town lattice design. In related history, the house adjacent to the bridge is the homestead of Dr. John Mott, philanthropist, Nobel peace prize winner and founder of the YMCA. The bridge had been closed for over a decade when restoration began in 1984. Only original construction techniques, methods and materials were used providing an authentic and complete restoration. All major components were reworked including the truss, chords, floor, roof, even the wooden pins (treenails) were made new and replaced. The work was accomplished by the Sullivan County Department of Public Works with technical assistance provided by noted covered bridge consultant Milton S. Graton of New Hampshire. The bridge was reopened in November 1985 and is listed on the National Register of Historic Places.

Yellow and blue New York State sign:

Livingston Manor Covered Bridge
Formerly Mott's Flat Bridge later known as
the "Vantran" original Towne lattice truss
built by John Davidson in 1860
Erected by Town of Rockland

Bendo

Rockland, Sullivan County

LOCATION: From Exit 96 off Route 17, go almost six miles east on County Route 82 to DeBruce, then two miles right on Willowemoc Road, then right to Covered Bridge Campsites and the bridge.

YEAR BUILT: 1860

TRUSS SYSTEM: Town

ROADWAY CARRIED: Conklin Hill Road

WATERWAY CROSSED: Willowemoc Creek

WEIGHT LIMIT: 3 tons

NUMBER OF SPANS: 1

LENGTH: 48'

CLEAR WIDTH: 11'-10"

OUT-TO-OUT WIDTH: 16'-4"

CLEARANCE: 8'-0"

BUILDER: John Davidson

OWNERSHIP: County

COVERED BRIDGE ASSIGNED NUMBER: NY-53–04

Field Observations

SIDES: Uniform and vertical siding

    Color: Natural wood and dark-brown stain

    Opening under eaves: Yes

    Flying buttresses: 4

      Location: 2 per side

      Height: Full

      End caps: Framework

    Ledges: None

PORTALS: Nonuniform and vertical siding

    Color: Natural wood and dark-brown stain

    Trim: None

    Overhang: 90 degrees

    Gables: Horizontal

FLOORING: Tire-track planking: Lengthwise

    Deck planking: Crosswise

ROOF: Metal

ABUTMENTS: North: Stone and mortar

    South: Concrete cap on top of steel shoring

WINGWALLS: NE & NW: Stone and mortar

    SE & SW: Stone fill

PIERS: None

WINDOWS: None

DOORS: None

SKEW ANGLE: 0 degrees

Newfield

Newfield, Tompkins County

LOCATION: Follow the signs from State Route 13 in the center of the village of Newfield.

YEAR BUILT: 1853

TRUSS SYSTEM: Town and Laminated Arch

ROADWAY CARRIED: Bridge Street

WATERWAY CROSSED: West Branch Cayuga Creek

WEIGHT LIMIT: 5 tons

NUMBER OF SPANS: 1

LENGTH: 115'

CLEAR WIDTH: 16'-0"

OUT-TO-OUT WIDTH: 19'-6"

CLEARANCE: 9'-5"

BUILDERS: Samuel Hamm and sons, David Dassance, and Patchen Parsons (carpenters); Benjamin Starr and Richard Russell (masons)

OWNERSHIP: Township

COVERED BRIDGE ASSIGNED NUMBER: NY-55–01

ABUTMENTS: Concrete caps on top of stone
  North: Stone fill
  South: Retaining wall

WINGWALLS: None

PIERS: None

WINDOWS: Number: 12
  Location: 6 per side
  Shape: Diamond
  Awnings: None

DOORS: None

SKEW ANGLE: 0 degrees

■ ■ ■

Yellow and brown sign on roof support:

Restored by M. S. Graton 1972

Bronze metal sign on east truss (south end):

Francesca Johnson met Robert Kincaid
August 16, 1963
D. Q. met his fair maiden
August 19, 1993
Their souls now dance on summer evenings
among the rafters of Roseman Bridge . . .
Newfield, N.Y.

Gold and silver metal sign on south gable:

Newfield Covered Bridge
Built 1853

Field Observations

SIDES: Uniform and horizontal siding
  Color: Barn red paint
  Opening under eaves: Yes
  Flying buttresses: None
    Ledges: 2
    Location: 1 per side
    Height: One-third of the way up from
      bottom
    Length: Full

PORTALS: Uniform and horizontal siding
  Color: Barn red paint
  Trim: None
  Overhang: Inward sloping from top
  Gables: Chamfered

FLOORING: Tire-track planking: None
  Deck planking: Lengthwise (middle three-fifths is
    treated)

ROOF: Shakes

Marie and Grant Musser Overlook
For their dedication to the preservation of
the Newfield Covered Bridge.

Marie and Grant Musser, long time residents of Tompkins County have actively pursued the preservation of the Newfield Covered Bridge since 1969. Their perseverance resulted in the restoration of the bridge in 1972 by Milton S. Graton, a nationally renowned preservationist. For their dedication and service, Marie and Grant were honored by the Tompkins County Board of Representatives on April 30, 1973 with an appointment as the "Keepers of the Covered Bridge," an appointment they still hold today. During the last 29 years the Musser's have selflessly made frequent and regular visits to the Covered Bridge ensuring that any necessary repairs were made in a timely and historically sensitive manner. Presented by Tompkins County and the Town of Newfield this eighth day of August 1998.

White and maroon Tompkins County sign:

Newfield Covered Bridge
Built in 1853 and dedicated to Elijah Moore, son of an early settler, this bridge is the oldest covered bridge in daily use in New York State. Constructed at a cost of $800.00, the distinctive diamond pattern of the "Town lattice truss" is pinned together with trunnels or "treenails." The roof and siding serve to protect the structure from the ravages of nature. Popular in the 1800's because of plentiful and inexpensive timber, covered bridges or "timber tunnels" became places for social gatherings. This is the only remaining covered bridge in Tompkins County.

Perrine's

Esopus and Rosendale, Ulster County

LOCATION: North of New Paltz on Route 32, turn east on Route 213 for 0.3 mile. The covered bridge sets next to the thruway bridge.

YEAR BUILT: 1844

TRUSS SYSTEM: Burr

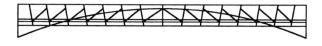

ROADWAY CARRIED: Bypassed section of Route 213

WATERWAY CROSSED: Wallkill River

WEIGHT LIMIT: Closed

NUMBER OF SPANS: 1

LENGTH: 154'

CLEAR WIDTH: 16'-5"

OUT-TO-OUT WIDTH: 19'-10"

CLEARANCE: 11'-0"

BUILDER: Benjamin West

OWNERSHIP: Township

COVERED BRIDGE ASSIGNED NUMBER: NY-56–01

Field Observations

SIDES: Nonuniform and vertical siding
  Color: Natural wood
  Opening under eaves: Yes
  Flying buttresses: None
  Ledges: None
PORTALS: Nonuniform and horizontal siding on
    gables
  Nonuniform and vertical siding on uprights
  Color: Natural wood
  Trim: None
  Overhang: 90 degrees
  Gables: Rounded
FLOORING: Tire-track planking: Crosswise
  Deck planking: Diagonal
ROOF: Wooden shingles
ABUTMENTS: Stone and mortar
WINGWALLS: Stone and mortar
PIERS: None
WINDOWS: None
DOORS: None
SKEW ANGLE: 0 degrees

■ ■ ■

Black and white sign on south gable:

Perrine's Bridge
Ulster County historical site circa 1844

Metal sign on left upright of south portal:

This valuable property was donated November 29, 1972 to the people of Ulster County
by the Culinarian's Home Foundation, Inc.
New York City

For use as a mini-park at the site of the historic
Perrine's Covered Bridge circa 1844
The second oldest covered bridge in New
York State
Ulster County legislature
Peter J. Savago, Chairman

Concrete Monument:

Perrine's Bridge Committee Officers
John Grady, President
Elmer Carney, Vice President
Clifford A. Henze, Treasurer
Thomas Orr, Secretary
Directors: Elmer Carney
Thomas Orr
Kenneth K. Clark
Mrs. Richard H. Priest
Allan S. Dargie
Harry Rigby, Jr.
Gerald Defelicis
Sol Rosenthal
John Grady
William Vanbenshoten
Clifford A. Henze
Walter G. Williams
Roger W. Mabie
Hon. Kenneth L. Wilson
Hugh McVey
Sherwood E. Davis, Counsel
Albert Edward Millikin, Consulting Architect
Bridge Erected—1850
Restored—1970
A historic site

Forge

Hardenbergh, Ulster County

LOCATION: From the bridge across Dry Brook on Route 28 in Arkville, take Dry Brook Road for almost 7.6 miles. Forge Covered Bridge sets next to Dry Brook Road. Permission is needed to visit this private bridge.

YEAR BUILT: 1906

TRUSS SYSTEM: Kingpost

ROADWAY CARRIED: Private

WATERWAY CROSSED: Dry Brook

WEIGHT LIMIT: Closed

NUMBER OF SPANS: 1

LENGTH: 27'
CLEAR WIDTH: 12'-9"
OUT-TO-OUT WIDTH: 14'-9"
CLEARANCE: 10'-0"
BUILDER: Jerome Moot
OWNERSHIP: Private
COVERED BRIDGE ASSIGNED NUMBER: NY-56–02

Field Observations

SIDES: Nonuniform and vertical siding
    Color: Natural wood
    Opening under eaves: No
    Flying buttresses: 6
        Location: 3 per side
        Height: Full
        End caps: Natural wood
    Ledges: None
PORTALS: Nonuniform and vertical siding

Color: Natural wood
Trim: None
Overhang: 90 degrees
Gables: Square
FLOORING: Tire-track planking: Lengthwise
    Deck planking: Crosswise
ROOF: Wooden shingles with metal ridge cap
ABUTMENTS: Stone
WINGWALLS: None
PIERS: None
WINDOWS: None
DOORS: None
SKEW ANGLE: 0 degrees

■ ■ ■

This is a private covered bridge with a wood fence across the east portal and posted with "No Trespassing" signs.

Tappan (Kittle)

Hardenbergh, Ulster County

LOCATION: From Forge Covered Bridge, take Dry Brook Road one mile south. The bridge is on Erickson Road.

YEAR BUILT: 1906

TRUSS SYSTEM: Kingpost (rebuilt without functional truss, 1985).

ROADWAY CARRIED: Erickson Road

WATERWAY CROSSED: Dry Brook

WEIGHT LIMIT: Unknown

NUMBER OF SPANS: 1

LENGTH: 43'

CLEAR WIDTH: 12'-4"

OUT-TO-OUT WIDTH: 14'-4"

CLEARANCE: 8'-3"

BUILDER: Jerome Moot

OWNERSHIP: Township

COVERED BRIDGE ASSIGNED NUMBER: NY-56–03

Field Observations

SIDES: Uniform and vertical siding

    Color: Natural wood

    Opening under eaves: No

    Flying buttresses: 6

        Location: 3 per side

        Height: Full

    End caps: Natural wood

    Ledges: None

PORTALS: Uniform and vertical siding

    Color: Natural wood

    Trim: None

    Overhang: 90 degrees

    Gables: Horizontal

FLOORING: Tire-track planking: Lengthwise

    Deck planking: Crosswise

ROOF: Wooden shingles with metal ridge cap

ABUTMENTS: Concrete

WINGWALLS: Concrete

PIERS: None

WINDOWS: None

DOORS: None

SKEW ANGLE: 0 degrees

Ashokan/Turnwood (New Paltz Campus, Olive)

Olive, Ulster County

LOCATION: Follow Route 213 through Olivebridge to Route 28A. Turn right for 1.5 miles, then right on Beaverkill Road for one mile. The gate will be on your right. Ask directions. There is a half-mile walk to the bridge. Permission is needed to view this private bridge.

YEAR BUILT: 1885

TRUSS SYSTEM: Town

ROADWAY CARRIED: Private

WATERWAY CROSSED: Esopus Creek

WEIGHT LIMIT: Closed

NUMBER OF SPANS: 1

LENGTH: 62'

CLEAR WIDTH: 13'-1"
OUT-TO-OUT WIDTH: 16'-5"
CLEARANCE: 10'-6"
BUILDER: Nelson Tompkins
OWNERSHIP: Private
COVERED BRIDGE ASSIGNED NUMBER: NY-56–05

Field Observations

SIDES: Nonuniform and vertical siding
Color: Natural wood
Opening under eaves: No
Flying buttresses: 4
Location: 2 per side
Height: Full
End caps: Natural wood
Ledges: None
PORTALS: Nonuniform and vertical siding
Color: Natural wood
Trim: None
Overhang: 90 degrees
Gables: Chamfered

FLOORING: Tire-track planking: None
Deck planking: Lengthwise
ROOF: Wooden shingles
ABUTMENTS: North: Concrete faced with stone
South: Cinder block and concrete faced with stone
WINGWALLS: None
PIERS: None
WINDOWS: 4
Location: 2 per side
Shape: Rectangular
Awnings: None
DOORS: None
SKEW ANGLE: 0 degrees

■　■　■

Black and white sign on both gables:

Ten dollars fine
Driving over this bridge
Faster than a walk

Grants Mills

Hardenbergh, Ulster County

LOCATION: From Forge Covered Bridge, go back about 1.5 miles to Mill Brook Road, turn left, and travel about five miles to the bridge. Or, from Route 28, take the back road on the south side of Pepacton Reservoir to Arena. Turn onto Mill Brook Road and go 6.5 miles to the bridge, found soon after crossing into Ulster County.

YEAR BUILT: 1902

TRUSS SYSTEM: Town

ROADWAY CARRIED: Bypassed section of Mill Brook Road

WATERWAY CROSSED: Mill Brook

WEIGHT LIMIT: Closed

NUMBER OF SPANS: 1

LENGTH: 66'

CLEAR WIDTH: 13'-10"

OUT-TO-OUT WIDTH: 17'-6"

CLEARANCE: 10'-0"

BUILDERS: Edgar Marks and Wesley Alton

OWNERSHIP: Township

COVERED BRIDGE ASSIGNED NUMBER: NY-56–06

Field Observations

SIDES: Uniform and vertical siding

    Color: Natural wood

    Opening under eaves: Yes

    Flying buttresses: 8

      Location: 4 per side

      Height: Full

      End caps: Shakes

    Ledges: None

PORTALS: Uniform and vertical siding

    Color: Natural wood

    Trim: None

    Overhang: 90 degrees

    Gables: Chamfered

FLOORING: Tire-track planking: None

    Deck planking: Crosswise

ROOF: Shakes

ABUTMENTS: Stone

WINGWALLS: None

PIERS: None

WINDOWS: 1

    Location: North side

    Shape: Rectangular

    Awnings: None

DOORS: None

SKEW ANGLE: 0 degrees

■　■　■

Gables: Green, red, and tan signs:

Grants Mills

–1902–

Uprights: Black and white signs:

10 ft. Clearance

Warning

6 Tons Safe Load

Plaque on west portal:

Grants Mills Covered Bridge
Built 1902 by Edgar Marks,
Wesley Alton, Orrin Marks.
Restored 1992 by Robert Marks,
Vredenburgh family and friends.

Eagleville

Jackson and Salem, Washington County

LOCATION: From Cambridge at intersection of Route 22 and Route 313, take Route 313 toward Vermont for 6 miles. Turn left onto Eagleville Road to the bridge.

YEAR BUILT: 1858

TRUSS SYSTEM: Town

ROADWAY CARRIED: Eagleville Road

WATERWAY CROSSED: Battenkill River

WEIGHT LIMIT: 3 tons

NUMBER OF SPANS: 1

LENGTH: 101'

CLEAR WIDTH: 13'-11"

OUT-TO-OUT WIDTH: 17'-3"

CLEARANCE: 8'-0"

BUILDER: Ephraim W. Clapp

OWNERSHIP: County

COVERED BRIDGE ASSIGNED NUMBER: NY-58–01

Field Observations

SIDES: Nonuniform and vertical siding

    Color: Light-brown paint

    Opening under eaves: No

    Flying buttresses: None

    Ledges: None

PORTALS: Nonuniform and vertical siding

    Color: White paint

    Trim: None

    Overhang: 90 degrees

    Gables: Chamfered

FLOORING: Tire-track planking: None

    Deck planking: Lengthwise with crosspieces

ROOF: Wooden shingles

ABUTMENTS: Concrete

WINGWALLS: Concrete

PIERS: None

WINDOWS: None

DOORS: 1

    Location: South side

SKEW ANGLE: 0 degrees

■ ■ ■

This covered bridge has inside weather boards.

Chain link fence was added to lower three-fourths of truss systems.

There is exterior metal armoring at both abutments.

Shushan

Jackson and Salem, Washington County

LOCATION: The bridge is in Shushan next to County Route 61.

YEAR BUILT: 1858

TRUSS SYSTEM: Town

ROADWAY CARRIED: Bypassed section of County Route 61

WATERWAY CROSSED: Battenkill River

WEIGHT LIMIT: Closed

NUMBER OF SPANS: 2

LENGTH: 161'

CLEAR WIDTH: 14'-6"

OUT-TO-OUT WIDTH: 18'-4"

CLEARANCE: 11'-3"

BUILDERS: Milton and James C. Stevens

OWNERSHIP: Private museum (nonprofit)
COVERED BRIDGE ASSIGNED NUMBER: NY-58–02

Field Observations

SIDES: Uniform and vertical siding
  Color: Dark-brown and reddish-brown paint
  Opening under eaves: No
  Flying buttresses: None
  Ledges: None
PORTALS: Nonuniform and horizontal siding
  Color: White paint
  Trim: None
  Overhang: 90 degrees
  Gables: Chamfered
FLOORING: Tire-track planking: None
  Deck planking: Lengthwise with crosspieces
ROOF: Metal
ABUTMENTS: East: Concrete
  West: Concrete pier
WINGWALLS: NE & SE: Concrete
PIERS: 1
  Type: Steel trestle on concrete footing
WINDOWS: 12
  Location: 5 per side and 2 in west portal (portal is
    enclosed)
  Shape: Diamond
  Awnings: None
DOORS: 3
  Location: 2 at east portal (entrance to museum)
    and 1 in west portal
SKEW ANGLE: 0 degrees

∎　∎　∎

This bridge is now a museum.
This covered bridge has inside weather boards.

Black and white sign on inside of west portal:

Shushan Covered Bridge
This 117 year old bridge the longest covered
span remaining on the Battenkill is being re-
stored by the Shushan Covered Bridge Ass'n
We need your help in this effort
Inquiries & Donations may be addressed to:
Shushan Covered Bridge Ass'n
Shushan, N.Y. 12873

Black letters on east portal:

1858
Five Dollars Fine for Rideing or Driveing on
this Bridge Faster than a Walk.

Black letters on right upright of east portal:

Hours: 1–5 PM
Season: Mem. Day W'k'd to July 4th: Sat.,
Sun. & Holidays
July 4th to Labor Day: Daily, Except Mon.
Labor Day to Colum. Day W'k'd: Sat., Sun.
& Holidays
Also Open by App't
Call 854–3870 or 854–3755

Black letters on west portal:

Five Dollars Fine for Rideing or Driveing on
this Bridge Faster than a Walk.

Rexleigh

Jackson and Salem, Washington County

LOCATION: From Salem, take Route 22 south for two miles, turn left on Rexleigh Road, and go 1.5 miles to the bridge.

YEAR BUILT: 1874

TRUSS SYSTEM: Howe

ROADWAY CARRIED: Rexleigh Road

WATERWAY CROSSED: Battenkill River

WEIGHT LIMIT: 3 tons

NUMBER OF SPANS: 1

LENGTH: 107'

CLEAR WIDTH: 13'-4"

OUT-TO-OUT WIDTH: 17'-10"

CLEARANCE: 12'-0"

BUILDERS: Reuben Comins (contractor and builder) and George Wadsworth (carpenter)
OWNERSHIP: County
COVERED BRIDGE ASSIGNED NUMBER: NY-58–03

Field Observations

SIDES: Uniform and vertical siding
    Color: Light-brown paint
    Opening under eaves: Yes
    Flying buttresses: None
    Ledges: None
PORTALS: Nonuniform and vertical siding
    Color: White paint
    Trim: None
    Overhang: 90 degrees
    Gables: Rounded
FLOORING: Tire-track planking: None
    Deck planking: Lengthwise
ROOF: Shakes
ABUTMENTS: East: Cut stone (white marble) on top
           of stone
    West: Concrete
WINGWALLS: NE & SE: Stone
    NW & SW: Concrete and stone fill
PIERS: None

WINDOWS: None
DOORS: 1
    Location: North side
SKEW ANGLE: 0 degrees

■   ■   ■

This covered bridge has inside weather boards. Chain-link fence was added to full height of truss systems.

Black letters on both gables:

Rexleigh Bridge
1874
25 Dollars Fine for Driving on this Bridge
Faster than a Walk.

Concrete monument:

Remove not the ancient landmark,
Which thy fathers have set.
Proverbs 22:28
Dedicated to the memory of Bernice Langlois
Whose love for our heritage
Helped save this covered bridge
For posterity.
1914–1983

Buskirk

Hoosic and White Creek, Rensselaer and Washington Counties

LOCATION: Buskirk is located on NYS Route 67 west of Eaglebridge. Take Washington County Route 103 from Route 67 north to the bridge in Buskirk.

YEAR BUILT: 1857

TRUSS SYSTEM: Howe

ROADWAY CARRIED: County Route 103 and County Route 59

WATERWAY CROSSED: Hoosic River

WEIGHT LIMIT: 6 tons

NUMBER OF SPANS: 1

LENGTH: 164'

CLEAR WIDTH: 16'-4"

OUT-TO-OUT WIDTH: 22'-4"

CLEARANCE: 10'-0"

BUILDERS: Peter O. Osterhauth, Charles Newman, and James B. Roberts (primary firm); Charles F. Ingalls (subcontractor)

OWNERSHIP: County
COVERED BRIDGE ASSIGNED NUMBERS:
   NY-42–02 and NY-58–04

Field Observations

SIDES: Nonuniform and vertical siding
   Color: Barn red paint
   Opening under eaves: Yes
   Flying buttresses: None
   Ledges: None
PORTALS: Nonuniform and vertical siding
   Color: Barn red paint
   Trim: White paint
   Overhang: 90 degrees
   Gables: Rounded
FLOORING: Tire-track planking: None
   Deck planking: Crosswise
ROOF: Shakes
ABUTMENTS: Concrete
WINGWALLS: Concrete
PIERS: None

WINDOWS: 12
   Location: 6 per side
   Shape: 5 rectangular and 1 square per side
   Awnings: Shakes
DOORS: None
SKEW ANGLE: 0 degrees

■   ■   ■

This covered bridge has inside weather boards.
White letters on both gables:

Buskirks Bridge
25 Dollars Fine for Driving on this Bridge
Faster than a Walk.

Yellow and blue New York State sign:

Buskirk's Red Covered Bridge
Built circa 1850 to replace a previous bridge
built in 1804. This crossing served the Great
Northern Turnpike beginning in 1799.
Erected 1979 by D. J. F

Appendix A

Appendix B

Appendix C

References

Index

APPENDIX A : Driving Distances Between Locations of Covered Bridges

Legend:

A. Downsville	F. Jay	K. Curry	P. Arkville	U. Salem
B. Delhi	G. Salisbury Center	L. Livingston Manor	Q. Olivebridge	V. Buskirk
C. Hamden	H. East Springfield	M. DeBruce	R. Arena	
D. Margaretville	I. Edinburg	N. Newfield	S. Cambridge	
E. Roscoe	J. North Blenheim	O. New Paltz	T. Shushan	

Driving Distances (miles)

	A	B	C	D	E	F	G	H	I	J	K	L	M	N	O	P	Q	R	S	T	U	V
A		22	16	23	28	259	112	87	115	61	45	25	30	104	76	38	53	24	162	177	174	148
B	22		11	21	66	260	90	58	117	34	60	40	45	107	86	32	52	24	127	142	139	114
C	16	11		27	32	252	100	69	119	44	54	34	39	101	85	35	58	27	138	153	150	137
D	23	21	27		50	237	100	78	93	30	71	56	58	119	58	1	31	6	115	114	126	108
E	28	66	32	50		276	132	110	142	79	22	7	8	112	56	50	73	44	146	153	176	139
F	259	260	252	237	276		177	197	129	196	255	270	268	275	230	237	227	243	182	127	122	175
G	112	90	100	100	132	177		41	75	71	147	142	146	154	152	114	153	115	91	98	95	94
H	87	58	69	78	110	197	41		58	42	113	117	122	129	110	81	109	81	98	94	91	87
I	115	117	119	93	142	129	75	58		63	148	163	161	194	123	93	121	98	88	54	66	81
J	61	34	44	30	79	196	71	42	63		66	72	77	130	83	36	44	37	93	98	95	80
K	45	60	54	71	22	255	147	113	148	66		19	12	148	37	36	51	44	138	150	149	125
L	25	40	34	56	7	270	142	117	163	72	19		7	129	54	36	67	36	155	166	166	142
M	30	45	39	58	8	268	146	122	161	77	12	7		133	52	41	65	40	154	165	164	140
N	104	107	101	119	112	275	154	129	194	130	148	129	133		180	134	156	120	213	218	214	200
O	76	86	85	58	56	230	152	110	123	83	37	54	52	180		59	28	67	113	125	124	100
P	38	32	35	1	50	237	114	81	93	36	36	36	41	134	59		31	14	130	145	142	116
Q	53	52	58	31	73	227	153	109	121	44	51	67	65	156	28	31		37	98	105	128	91
R	24	24	27	6	44	243	115	81	98	37	44	36	40	120	67	14	37		130	146	143	117
S	162	127	138	115	146	182	91	98	88	93	138	155	154	213	113	130	98	130		10	12	8
T	177	142	153	114	153	127	98	94	54	98	150	166	165	218	125	145	105	146	10		4	20
U	174	139	150	126	176	122	95	91	66	95	149	166	164	214	124	142	128	143	12	4		20
V	148	114	137	108	139	175	94	87	81	80	125	142	140	200	100	116	91	117	8	20	20	

APPENDIX B: Year Built, Length, Clearance, and Weight Limit

Bridges by Year Built

1. Hyde Hall (1823)
2. Perrine's (1844)
3. Newfield (1853)
4. Downsville (1854)
5. Blenheim (1855)
6. Buskirk (1857)
7. Jay (1857)
8. Eagleville (1858)
9. Shushan (1858)
10. Hamden (1859)
11. Bendo (1860)
12. Van Tran Flat (1860)
13. Beaverkill (1865)
14. Fitch's (1870)
15. Tuscarora Club (1870)
16. Rexleigh (1874)
17. Salisbury Center (1875)
18. Lower Shavertown (1877)
19. Copeland (1879)
20. Ashokan/Turnwood (1885)
21. Grants Mills (1902)
22. Forge (1906)
23. Tappan (1906)
24. Halls Mills (1912)

Bridges by Length (feet)

1. Forge (27)
2. Lower Shavertown (32)
3. Copeland (35)
4. Tuscarora Club (38)
5. Tappan (43)
6. Bendo (48)
7. Salisbury Center (50)
8. Hyde Hall (53)
9. Ashokan/Turnwood (62)
10. Grants Mills (66)
11. Beaverkill (98)
12. Eagleville (101)
13. Rexleigh (107)
14. Fitch's (100)
15. Newfield (115)
16. Van Tran Flat (117)
17. Halls Mills (130)
18. Hamden (130)
19. Perrine's (154)
20. Shushan (161)
21. Buskirk (164)
22. Downsville (174)
23. Jay (175)
24. Blenheim (228)

Bridges Still in Daily Use by Clearance (feet and inches)

1. Downsville (6'-0")
2. Beaverkill (6'-6")
3. Salisbury Center (7'-6")
4. Van Tran Flat (7'-8")
5. Bendo (8'-0")
6. Eagleville (8'-0")
7. Tappan (8'-3")
8. Fitch's (9'-0")
9. Hamden (9'-0")
10. Newfield (9'-5")
11. Buskirk (10'-0")
12. Lower Shavertown (11'-6")
13. Rexleigh (12'-0")

Bridges Still in Daily Use by Weight Limit (tons)

1. Beaverkill (3 tons)
2. Bendo (3 tons)
3. Downsville (3 tons)
4. Eagleville (3 tons)
5. Fitch's (3 tons)

6. Hamden (3 tons)
7. Rexleigh (3 tons)
8. Salisbury Center (3 tons)
9. Newfield (5 tons)

10. Van Tran Flat (5 tons)
11. Buskirk (6 tons)
12. Lower Shavertown (unknown)
13. Tappan (unknown)

APPENDIX C: Covered Bridges Listed on the National Register of Historic Places

1. Blenheim 10/15/66
2. Salisbury Center 6/19/72
3. Perrine's 4/13/73
4. Buskirk 3/8/78
5. Eagleville 3/8/78
6. Rexleigh 3/8/78
7. Shushan 3/8/78
8. Copeland 8/6/98
9. Grants Mills 12/17/98
10. Hyde Hall 12/17/98
11. Downsville 4/29/99
12. Fitch's 4/29/99
13. Hamden 4/29/99
14. Lower Shavertown 4/29/99
15. Newfield 2/25/00
16. Ashokan/Turnwood 7/20/00

References

Allen, R. 1991. "Batten Kill Bridges." *Empire State Courier* 26 (1): 3–7.

Bivins, M. 1999. "Discover Our Bridges to the Past." *Explore Our Town— A Guide to Roscoe & Livingston Manor* 8 (1): 8.

"Cooper, James Fenimore." 1995. *Microsoft Encarta '95.* CD-ROM.

Covered Bridges in New York State. N.d. Rome, N.Y.: New York State Covered Bridge Society.

Galusha, D. 1989. "Wood Over Water." *Catskill Center Newsletter* Spring): 8–9.

Glimmerglass State Park. N.d. Cooperstown, N.Y.: State of New York Office of Parks, Recreation, and Historic Preservation.

Guay, D. 1999. "Downsville Covered Bridge Dedication May 22, 1999." *Empire State Courier* 34 (2): 6–7.

Helsel, Bill, ed. 1989. *World Guide to Covered Bridges.* Rev. ed. Marlboro, Mass.: National Society for the Preservation of Covered Bridges.

Herrmann, W. 1974. *Spans of Time—Covered Bridges of Delaware County, N.Y.* Delhi, N.Y.: Delside Press, 42, 108, 110–11.

Jeffrey, A. 1999. "Covered Bridge Mailbox." *New York State Covered Bridge Society Newsletter* (May 9).

McKee, B. 1997. *Historic American Covered Bridges.* New York: Oxford University Press, 64.

Michielsen, J., and B. Michielsen. 1998. "Salisbury Covered Bridge Days." *Empire State Courier* 33 (3): 2–3.

Miller, Patricia B. 1977. *Timbers of Time.* Arkville, N.Y.: Erpf Catskill Cultural Center, 28–32.

Munson, R. 1992. "Dedication of Grants Mills Covered Bridge." *Empire State Courier* 27 (3): 3–6.

Raymond, R. 1995. "Age Finally Determined for the Buskirk Covered Bridge." *Empire State Courier* 30 (1): 8.

Rinda, W. 1999. "Rebirth of the Downsville Bridge." *Empire State Courier* 34 (1): 3–4.

Shushan Covered Bridge Museum. N.d. Shushan, N.Y.: Shushan Covered Bridge Association.

Sloane, E. 1954. *American Barns and Covered Bridges.* New York: Wilfred Funk, 102–4.

United States National Park Service. 2000. *About the National Register of Historic Places.* ParkNet. http://www.cr.nps.gov/nr/about.htm.

Wells, P. 1996. "Last Covered Bridge in the North Country: Historic Past and Uncertain Future." *Empire State Courier* 31 (1): 3–5.

Wilson, R. 1976. "Bridge Report." *Empire State Courier* 11 (3): 5.

Wilson, R. 1991a. "25 Year Anniversary Bonus Issue." *Empire State Courier* 26 (1): 14–16.

Wilson, R. 1991b. "Campbell's Bridge." *Empire State Courier* 26 (3): 8.

Wilson, R. 1997. "What Happened at Jay." *Empire State Courier* 32 (3): 2.

Wilson, R. 1999. Telephone interview with author, 19 September.

Index

Italic page number denotes photograph.